THINGS THAT BURN

Things That Burn

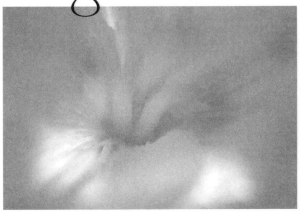

JACQUELINE BERGER

THE UNIVERSITY
OF UTAH PRESS
Salt Lake City

09 08 07 06 05   5 4 3 2 1

 The Defiance House Man colophon is a registered trademark
of the University of Utah Press. It is based upon a four-foot-tall,
Ancient Puebloan pictograph (late PIII) near Glen Canyon, Utah.

LIBRARY OF CONGRESS CATALOGING-IN-PUBLICATION DATA

Berger, Jacqueline, 1960
Things that burn / Jacqueline Berger.
p. cm.
ISBN 0-87480-827-8 (pbk. : alk. paper)
I. Title.
PS3602.E7538T48 2005
811'.6—dc22   2004025991

FOR JEFF

CONTENTS

III

IV

I

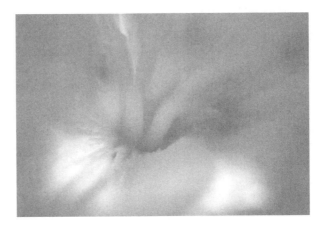

Prayer

Even those of us who don't believe
or don't know what to believe in
know enough to frame it as request.
Please we whisper in our minds,
sitting beside the hospital bed
where your mother, unconscious
since they opened her heart,
is fighting to come back.
Please we plead with the emptiness
because what else is there
to say into the night sky
on the long drive from the hospital
back up the mountain to your parents' house.
To the stars burning in the trees,
please, and to the black snake of the road,
and to the heat the next morning already rising
off the deck where your aunts
have gathered to smoke.
Please to the drive back down the mountain,
to the landmarks I memorize
to gauge the distance: the Sloughhouse fruit stand
whose corn was so sweet when we cooked it
the other night it needed no butter or salt.
Please to the small river and then the large river

we cross before the left turn at Felix's Spy Shop

with its tools of surveillance

whose customers must so want to be safe

they stalk. *Please* to the Burger Chief

where the next turn comes,

its faded awning a kind of flag to get ready.

And now into the parking lot and out of the car,

a wall of heat as we cross and then the cold air

of the hospital and up to the ICU on the fourth floor

where everything we know of life—

how much we want it, how much

it makes us suffer—

is there on your mother's face,

mouth open, eyes wandering and then shut.

Last night your brother heard her

tell the nurse *save me,*

low but clear.

We want everything to be okay,

but we also want our hearts to be broken

and in that brokenness to be lifted

out of the smallness of our lives.

And so *please* to the sweetness of grief

that makes us finally want to know our parents

and let them know us.

Please to whomever can be appealed to

for help, *please* to the strangeness of beauty,

to the poison oleander that lines the highway

and to the vineyards that grow on hillsides
in their sloped grace. To the single-lane roads
and to the train of cars behind us,
all of them anxious as well to arrive.
Please to the past we cannot let go of
with its lovers like a ballroom of ghosts.
Please to the future we walk into blindfolded.
Please to the body's invisible work
of repair, to the heart and the liver,
to the kidneys and the brain
the night the doctors tell us your mother
may not find her way back
from whatever dark place she is lost to.
Later she will say those days were dreams
of being tied in ropes.
And yes, *please* to the way sorrow throws us
into each other, my life into yours
and into your family's,
and back into my own,
the hard way we begin to belong.

GOOD THURSDAY

Rushed out of the house
to get to my group across the bridge,
and you off to watch the game with my ex.
You grab a bottle of wine on your way out,
kiss me, and now I'm alone
in the small world of my car.
It is almost winter.
After the long light of summer,
early dark arrives like unaccounted sadness.
I drive through it,
random thoughts of food and money,
something about the weekend,
then a song I recognize but cannot name
comes on the radio and I feel some opening
in that part of the mind that governs longing
and nostalgia—the smell of a lover's house
long ago when I let myself in
with the key he gave me
those first months when desire—
what is there new to say about desire?
The song is over.
You have probably arrived by now,
the TV is on and you are on the floor
scratching the dog's belly while my ex

opens the wine and hands you a glass.

I will soon be in Sharon's living room,

taking off my coat, filling a bowl with popcorn,

trying to say something true.

It is a fine life, a good Thursday.

I wanted once to be torn apart by love,

ground to powder

and flung like a handful of stars

into the night sky.

To say I miss that feeling

is not to say I want it back.

Tonight the moon is an orange disk on the horizon.

I want to put it between my teeth,

let it dissolve on my tongue,

let the river of the moon trickle into me.

I want to glow with the orange light of the moon

in honor of love—

great love, hard love,

love torn open,

all of its edges frayed.

And then the thread of love,

the white stitching

on the midnight blue of love,

a constellation of weekdays,

the Thursday of love, the Friday,

what I come home to

as well as what I have said

I will live without.

THE WARMEST DAY OF THE YEAR

The war has entered the marketplace
of a country where women must choose
whether it is worth the risk
to buy more fruit and bread,
sugar for tea, cigarettes, soap.
All I did today was refuse
to buy the stamps with the flag.
In line at the post office,
the man behind me asked if I had a child
at the university
named on my envelope.
I'm not old enough to have a child in college
I said in a tone I hoped would embarrass.
Then later, driving away, I thought how stupid—
of course I'm old enough.
I could have a child in the war
like the boys I read about this morning—
nineteen, twenty, twenty-two—
who love the rush of battle,
I can't imagine
being in a line of work that didn't
let me carry a gun,
one of them said, though quick to add,

I hate to kill, and *it's for a cause.*
One of these boys could be mine.
I could have stared at him across the dinner table
in the weeks before he left,
trying to memorize his face,
to understand how the corners of his mouth
tilt upward, to know the birthmark next to his ear
as well as I know the blow of his joining
an institution my whole heart is set against.

I have one child in college
and one in the war
I tell the man in line as I drive through town,
and I live for awhile in that other life.
How would I not favor the one child
over the other? But perhaps I always have
and so the one who—and how could he not—
sensed my displeasure did the thing he knew
would displease me most.

Kill the children who will grow up to be soldiers,
wrote the Greeks of their Trojan enemies.
Kill the women who make men soft,
imagining the life they could go home to.
A culture devoted to logic.
Science dismantles the miraculous,
wrote Hippocrates.

But if it is knowledge that makes the world unholy,

we should be bent in prayer

for the little we know of our lives.

The string section adds the almost human

sound of weeping to the symphony.

Often I fail to hear the layered

nuance of sound

and fall asleep at concerts.

Listen to the birds and the dogs,

said my lover on the first night of the bombing.

On TV we saw the sky lit and heard,

between explosions, mad chirping

and the distant howls of pets or strays.

THE WORK

How do you try to present yourself
in writing, asked a writer friend,
a question I keep coming back to.
Van Gogh told Theo in a letter
not to worry about greatness,
just work on getting true
the face, the torso, the wheat field
in the last hour of winter light.

Maybe it is easier for painters,
they have something to look at
and oil, charcoal, chalk
to put between themselves
and the thing they are making.
But writers are bunched
in the crowded room of the mind
with only language for company.

In the alumni review
people far from their college days
were asked about their favorite teachers.
A man said: He was a professor I hated.
For an entire semester we sketched
the head of David.

One sketch after another
my teacher rejected—
too studied, lacks breath—
until finally I dashed one off.
This one, said my teacher,
is genuine.
Then he tore it to pieces.
Don't love your work
he told me, but love
that you *can* work
and come back each day
to that blankness.

Maybe this is the problem,
we confuse *work* and *last.*
It didn't work out
we told each other,
but we meant
it didn't last.

Sketch after sketch of your body
made by my eyes
then crumpled and tossed into the fire.
How beautiful you looked in underwear,
I couldn't believe you were mine.
Of course it didn't last,
how long can any of us hold
a branch of burning blossoms?

How do I try to present myself?

Naked, but with good lighting.

As when the moon, just past full,

silvers the sky

or when the sun at the last

of a clear day in January

turns the houses on the hillside

into squares of gold.

Or when you looked at me, sometimes,

from so far into the fields of love

I responded by undressing even further.

The Hungers

My dog would like to be huge,
the fattest spaniel ever.
He is satisfied when he sits on his pillow
after his biscuit,
but he would be more satisfied
eating himself to death.
I imagine him one hundred pounds,
Guinness-record size,
photographed on a pedestal, a garland
of lilies 'round his neck.
His is a pure desire.
I am meek in comparison, though curious.
Do you think I could get to two hundred?
I ask my beloved. He puts his own number
at three-fifty.

An actor starved himself to play a man
hiding in his own city during war,
city in which in happier times he had eaten
pastries made with sweet cheese and glazed fruit,
apple in winter, apricot in summer.
His body, he told the interviewer,
would drop no lower than one-thirty.
I'm six foot one, he said, I would have
kept going. They shot in reverse order,

so the actor first stood in his wasted body
before the camera then gradually
gained back the weight until
he looked like his character
before the war, lean to begin with,
a loner who lived for music.
The act of starving changed the way
he looked at lace curtains,
steam heat, the comfort
of a life about to end.

I put my low at seventy.
After that, I would probably die.
I am not like the anorexic
who believes she can walk through walls,
no number too small:
forty pounds, twenty, ten,
until she is a bottle of water,
then a bracelet, a thimble, a ring.
Bypassing death, the body
in her cosmology can be willed
into feather, thread,
can be unraveled.

Admit that you are powerless over food.
My beloved is on the bed, his blue robe
has come open and I see his round belly
and soft penis. He is reading step one.

I have, he continues, *stolen and lied,*
compromised friendships, eaten garbage,
and maimed my body. Maimed?
we both ask, as though our digits
were Vienna sausages.
I laugh until I pee my pants a little
and have to blow dry the crotch
because I am getting ready to go out
and don't want to change my clothes.
I love that I can make you wet,
he says. Later I buy a cake for a party,
chocolate, because the one man
who will eat it without guilt
likes chocolate.

My dog wants to be huge
because that would mean
he always gets what he wants.
I prefer to be small
because I do not want
to get what I want.
The cake in the box poses a question:
Can you give up desire without giving up
the objects of desire?
But without desire, what is cake
but flour and sugar and the powder
of a bean too bitter in its natural state to eat.
The cake is a hand mirror

in whose dark light the soul swims

in currents going first one and then

the other direction.

Must there not, even in the midst of horror,

have been some moment when a woman,

half way between life and death

in the camps or in hiding,

looked at herself and thought, ironically,

this is the body I have always wanted

before it began to vanish.

Lexicon

The language in my mouth
comes from academies I would never,
as a girl, have been allowed to enter,
in centuries when no one in my family
knew how to read.
It comes from coffee houses in London
when the craving for caffeine
changed the map of the world,
a craving around which empires
were erected or dismantled.
It comes from clubs and reading rooms,
libraries and halls,
the lexicon like the fork of a river
that over time mixed with the family pool
and turned us from dark to fair,
as the family itself, over time,
learned to untwist the damp ropes
of the ruler's language,
so even now a book of philosophy
is floating somewhere in Poland
years after my great uncle wrote it
and years after he was loaded with the others
onto a train and on some winter midnight
was hauled out from under the worn blanket of sleep,

was dragged to a field and shot,

the blood pulled like a handkerchief

from his breast pocket,

the warmth of it melting a small section of snow.

In my mouth is the figs in syrup

drizzled with cream of the officers' meal,

and the whole bird carved into,

and the sage-scented steam it releases.

In my mouth is the black blood of a Jew

dying on his knees,

is the bread a woman stuffs in her mouth

while clearing the table

after the generals have gone off to smoke.

In my mouth is the knotted silk

a man slips between his lover's teeth

to muffle the sorrowful orchestra of pleasure.

PORTRAIT OF MY PARENTS

My parents are standing in the shallow end
of the slow lane at the Westside Y.
My father is wearing a swimmer's cap
whose peak, like a satin yarmulke, won't stay flat.
My mother is wearing a shower cap.
I would like to paint my parents standing there,
visible from the shoulders up.
They are talking about dinner
and what we have to buy at the market.
In the painting I would suggest
through color and shading
the ordinary intimacy of closeness,
or how my parents suddenly look like old Jews,
though I don't remember them aging.
My canvas would have a background of tile,
white and slick.
I would loosely sketch the straps
of my mother's suit, my father's
rounded shoulders, the slope
of their bodies into water.
Then I would paint the sweetness
of my parents, good people
whose failures sadden them.
I would paint the water

and what is blurred beneath it.

My parents are still standing there, talking.

I wave to them, one lane over,

as I swim past.

Then my mother is on her side,

gliding out into the deep end,

careful to keep her head above water,

and my father follows, doing the crawl,

his head turning from side to side

as he breathes.

UNDER THE SURFACE

I don't remember most of my life,
if I tally up the minutes,
the days when nothing happened—
I ran into the store for apples or milk,
opened the door to let the dog out or in,
the moon arrived in its rowboat
either early or late,
things that slide off the greased surface
of memory without a trace.
We remember repetition,
the road we took every day for the five years
we lived in the little house on the corner,
but also tragedy or joy,
moments so singular they rise above
the dark pond of the past
and gleam in the twilight like golden rafts
at the height of summer.
What I love is when something
I haven't thought about in years
returns, intact, and down to the smallest detail.
These memories are like fish,
alive, but locked below the frozen
surface of the lake.
What is the self that carries so much

of what it doesn't use but can't bear to give away?

Somewhere is every postcard I ever received,

old report cards, and the certificate

from the summer I learned to swim.

It took until August

but finally I graduated

from *Porpoises* to *Sharks.*

How to Be Happy

I've had good times
and even long stretches
when my life seemed to hum along:
prizes and lovers
like it was my turn,
standing with my dress gathered up like a net
to catch windfall, a strong breeze
and the trees laden with fruit.
It passes, that lucky streak,
but beyond that, happy
like standing in light,
like the whole of the mind illuminated,
all twelve billion neurons whistling
the same snappy tune,
that kind of happy comes in moments
so brief and stunning they leave us reeling.
Once in the arms of a lover,
standing on a hill, the day bright
and cool, I felt the burden
of myself lift and the whole family
of cells inside me flood their banks with joy.
You levitate a little being that happy.
You lose yourself, no part left behind
thinking, I am happy.

You and happy are the same,

a state of being,

and the grizzled note taker

who keeps track of your life

is temporarily relieved of her duty.

But almost as soon as you have entered

happiness's grand ballroom

and swept its marble floor with your skirts

you are out again.

The dancers become memory,

the gossamer of their dresses, the glide,

something you will recall

from time to time as you stand

in the hallway listening

for the faint music of the orchestra.

STRANGE ANIMAL THAT KNOWS SO MANY TRICKS

If I think of the mind as a container,
a perfume bottle of amber liquid,
old fashioned, with gold flakes
that flurry when you shake the bottle
then fall like snow
when you set it back on the bureau,
if I think of the mind like this,
I can feel sweet fondness for its ways.
But sometimes the mind is a dog
with a chewing problem
working its way through a wooden gate.
Never mind the belly of splinters,
it imagines running free
through a city of danger and joy
and will stop at nothing until it gets there.
I have spent whole days
thinking of the one thing
that torments me most.
At such times my mind
feels like something attached,
a Siamese twin I drag through life
wishing I could saw her off.
Can the mind solve the problems
the mind creates?

It believes it can and makes equations,

hypotheses, theorems,

each one leading deeper in.

It must be another department

that nightly recasts

the mathematical as myth,

producing in sleep

the boulevards of childhood,

trees that sing, the sun

burning a hole in the paper sky.

ALL OF IT

I want to love my life
though it is easier to brood
over what I have wasted.
I wasted my twenties,
hoarding the body's pleasures
when I should have splurged.
I should have had an affair
with the Spanish tennis star
but I didn't believe beauty
could be anything but mocking.
Twenty-six would have been
the perfect year to go to bars
with a boy like that.
I am trying to love my life
even as I see how much of it
I refused to live.
But the refusal is also the life.
I want to love its dim rooms
and the tenderness of solitude,
the bruised plum.
I am trying to love my thirties
when the great moment of love
finally arrived but in the end
I could not hold it.

I want to love winter
when the only light in the woods
comes from a moon hidden in fog.
I want to cherish the time
of my life and the small boat
of the body I ride across it in.
I want to love where I am now,
every choice informed by loss.
And I want to love the rest
of my life that every day gets shorter,
each day fed to the past by evening.
I want to love that too.
My life diminished
and radiant in the rubbing away.

II

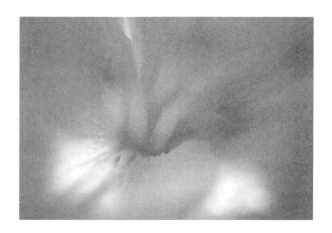

DRIVING UNDER THE INFLUENCE

The second most popular place

after the house

for private eating is the car.

The right hand in a blur of movement

from bag to mouth

mimics the car itself

eating the road,

speeding to its destination.

There are easy things to eat

one-handed while driving:

crackers, an apple, cookies, a sandwich,

and hard things: pasta salad,

a dish of ice cream.

Imagine you are out where the highway

heads to the sea, the sky is large,

traffic is light, and your favorite tape

is playing the song you love most.

Now you are alone in a way

that is harder in a room, alone

in the vastness of the mind,

your whole life spread before you.

Eating is part of this pleasure,

the umbilical that connects

the invisible sky of the mind

to the plain pasture of the body.

It's funny, in an anthology of poems
about driving—the road
is the true American architecture—
no one writes about eating in cars.
There's cars and music, naturally,
and cars and sex, both the fumbling
first attempts and the nostalgic sex
of long marrieds parking by the lake,
the lights twinkling on the distant shore.
There are poems about cars and cigarettes,
and cars and friends, and famous fights,
and cars and thoughts of dying,
and of driving until you get to a place
where no one knows you,
and of dogs riding shotgun,
and of gun racks and deer and elk
stiff on the roof.
But eating is suspiciously absent
among the acts that accompany
the transport of the body through space.

It embarrasses,
the desire to be alone
and do this thing
that takes you both close,
the intimacy of feeding,
and far, the mind

miles away from the animal

at the trough.

And yet it is the mind

that cries for more.

The body is easy to fill,

the mind never

gets enough.

Poets love the stuff by the side of the road:

dead animals, an abandoned shopping cart

in the middle of nowhere—

notes in the margin.

But consider Mom's care package

on the seat beside you,

cold chicken wrapped in foil,

chocolate cake, a thermos of coffee.

How long does it take,

one town over or not even,

until your fingers begin to undress the lovelies

and your mouth

opens to be filled?

THE CITY IS A MOVIE

Driving across town,
twilight's deep blue
blurs the buildings
while traffic lights,
suspended, shimmer.
In the Mission District the awnings
are rolled up for the night,
green pears, red bananas,
pomegranates covered in plastic.
On the radio there's a story
about a museum in Germany
exhibiting cadavers
slit open and preserved.
The surgeon-turned-artist has arranged
the bodies so they appear to be juggling
their own parts like plates.
Strung on invisible wires,
livers and lungs leap from the body
and muscles jump airborne
like planes lifting off the runway.
The curator tells the American interviewer
that Germans see through the eyes of guilt
and are willing to test the limits

of tolerance, hence the record crowds
attending the museum this first
weekend of spring.
At the stoplight I glance over
at a young couple embracing
in bulky jackets against a building.
I stay on them a second longer
and see the familiar thrust.
I imagine the girl
going along with this,
not exactly against her will
but beside it,
separated from it,
though who knows,
maybe it was she who unzipped
the boy's jeans,
hardening his cock in her hands.
The light turns and I'm into
the next neighborhood, more upscale
with its dry cleaners and bookstores
and on the radio a holistic nutritionist
is talking about diet.
We Live Our Lives in Bodies
is the title of a book
I saw advertised
in a literary journal

and though I didn't
order the volume
of poems, I imagine
it addressed the impossible bridge
of flesh that love
and fear must cross.

LETTERS FROM HOME

The other night in bed with a boy
so new to manhood the hair
on his body was downy,
I was gentle, wanting
more but holding back
for the sake of his innocence.
And only last night a rat
in love with his mother
ran after her when, uncaged,
she whipped the floor with her tail.
He shit in his excitement,
one or two pellets of joy,
then ate them
as animals sometimes do.
The other animals in my dream
last night were dogs
lying at the bottom of a swimming pool.
I recognized my spaniel and watched
to see his breathing.
What I love about myself,
unconscious, is how willing
I am to know nothing.
Dogs sleep underwater?
Well, okay.

Sons love their mothers like rats,

and boys young enough to be my children

rub the silk of their chests

against me, the tenderness

of flesh held like a handful of milkweed.

The mind has a mind of its own.

Prolific dreamer, filling

pages with a reckless hand.

She leaves the epistles on the bureau

for me to find in the morning.

Her style so different from mine,

what does she care

about morals or the tedious

limits of matter?

She titles the packet *Letters from Home*,

a frontier land of outlandish

displays, the only rule

to tongue the speech

of truth, and twist it.

EATING IN PUBLIC

The man across the aisle on the train—
we are headed to Chicago, outside
light drizzle, dull towns—
has wild hair the color of steel,
a bulky suit. He's jowly
with a long raspberry birthmark
like a string of drool
from the corner of his mouth.
He's eating a bagel sandwich,
chewing robustly, picking his teeth.
I understand why poetry
articulates longing
more easily than fulfillment.
Hunger is easy.
Desire is an open window with the light
pouring through, the body lit
and the bones shining like rods.
But satiety, thick fingered,
fumbles in the dark
its private pleasure.
I'm like any woman
with an empty tray
standing in front of a row of cakes
arranged on little plates.

My heart, a pendulum,

swings between two truths,

I want everything, I am ashamed

to want at all.

I would like to be invisible

when I carry my selection back to the table.

But I love to watch others

eating in public.

I am in awe of the simple naming of need

and the plain impulse to fill it.

The Student

It's hard to say how old he is,
maybe fifty or sixty,
my guess is younger
than he looks.
Worn thin, and add to that
slightly aggressive,
drawn to the contrary
yet alongside this
a nervous desire to please.
For three weeks he sat in the front row
drinking from a bottle
wrapped in a bag
and I saw nothing.
Long practice in making normal
the constant unraveling,
he knows how to be invisible.
Another student finally came and told me.

I used to blame my mother
years after the fact
for failing to notice
my teenage self
cutting skin, refusing
or devouring food.

What is the agreement
between two people
that makes what is there,
not there?
I was never caught
is one way of looking at it.
Another is that no one saw
a girl with good attendance
falling apart.

When I confronted my student
in the empty room after class,
he didn't deny it
and looked more lost than guilty,
chose as his strategy
playing dumb:
other students drink in class,
referring to the plastic bottles on the desks
as though it were a simple matter of taste,
some like water, others prefer vodka.
This is what it is like
to lie down in the warm puddle of shame,
to let it seep all the way into you.
I wanted to crowd in next to him,
huddled close so we both could fit.
Part of our agreement
was that if he left class

he wouldn't come back five minutes later—
I imagined him taking a quick slug
behind the building—
but would go home instead,
that day over.
I worried when he didn't show
and at the same time felt relieved.
In the end he sailed across
the finish line with an A,
his final paper an argument to reconcile
science and faith.
It's no longer true
that everything real
can be proven,
long gone is Newton's measurable universe,
and God knows it takes more
than gears and pulleys
to get us through the day.

EVENING NEWS

A girl who looks sixteen
is holding her son in her arms,
feeding him a bottle
and answering questions about her husband
who is missing or captive.
She doesn't understand the word *nature.*
What is the nature of the work
your husband does?
She doesn't understand how it came to be
that a news team is in her yard,
that her getting pregnant
and their getting married—
I'm imagining here and maybe unfairly—
and his joining the service so they'd have
some kind of future
could lead to this.
Suddenly the whole war
is her fault
and the terrible thought I have
is of taking her son—
why wait until he is eighteen—
and killing him now.
Toss him in the air
and shoot him.

The girl fills the screen

with her bland expression,

answering the questions as though

she were on trial,

as though she figured out

somewhere along the line

that giving away as little as you can

is the best way to stay out of trouble.

What does her husband do

is how the reporter rephrases the question.

Mechanic.

Her baby is good, doesn't wake or fuss.

She could be a student of mine,

a girl who stays in the back,

who never, the whole semester,

comes to see me though each paper

of hers I return has the same note

next to the low grade: come to an office hour,

get extra help.

The girl is an easy target,

the simplest one to hate.

I feel as though I know her,

as though I were the one

who had failed her.

THE SQUARE OF GRIEF

I don't know what it would be like
to be poor and sixteen and carry a gun
with the intention, before the night is out,
of using it, and on whom matters less
than the fact of pulling the trigger
and watching someone crumble
in the terror that precedes the bullet.
I am not a boy who has been told
his whole life that he is nothing
and that his life is nothing,
that if it were lifted onto a scale and weighed
it would not even make the needle move,
but I do know something about rage
and the grief that lives beneath it.
If I were that boy I might be moved to see the logic
in getting a gun and finding someone
walking home with a bag of groceries
lightly swinging by her side,
and I might be the one who came between
that woman and her next step,
the one who shot her for the five dollars
she had in her pocket.
The feeling that someone must pay,
must provide the soft ground

for the hard rain to pour into,

that feeling is not incomprehensible to me.

I wonder if this is what drove my friend's husband

and the other boys in the story

he told us one night over dinner and a few beers

to corner the girl and do to her

what he still doesn't call

in his own mind, rape.

She was a slut and they,

the boys, were childhood friends,

the year was 1962,

the innocence of the time somehow

absolving the boys of guilt.

And the girl, what did she do?

Girls have a way of exacting payment

from their own bodies, carving

into their skin the way one might whittle

a bar of soap or a piece of wood to pass the time.

A boy might get a gun, but a girl

prefers the slow blood that rises

from the knife.

My friend is the one who was shot

and the boy who did it,

because he was only a boy,

sixteen at the most, but maybe

only fourteen, or twelve and a half

and tall for his age, the boy

was never caught,

though who's to say,

by now he may be locked in a cell,

the rest of his life spent pacing

the square of grief

and the border of rage that surrounds it.

THINGS THAT BURN

I was talking to my friend last night about violence,

not the real kind that ends up on the news,

but violence chiseled into art.

If the imagery is there in us,

it is ours to use

was my point, more or less.

But it's too easy, works too well,

was hers. Besides which,

why add to the litany of suffering?

At some point one of us mentioned

O'Keeffe's flowers,

their obsessive petals burning

orange and purple to the edge of the canvas.

I started thinking about arroyos

full of water, silver rivers

under the milky eye of the moon.

Then arroyos full of bones, powdery

as ground light, skulls and femurs

of the palest grey and blue.

We don't choose what lives in us,

the best we can do is walk in the direction

of its heat. A man slings his leg over the balcony,

then, quick, he's in the bedroom.

The girl jumps up, tries to run

but his hand catches the ruffle

of her nightgown

before the dream sputters

and the lights come on.

Violence and arroyos full of wild flowers

burning like a boat of color

are two currents merging.

My friend suggested that I try to talk

to the man, *Before you fall asleep*

prepare what you want to say.

Later we watched a video,

Red Riding Hood as you've never seen her

it said on the box.

I love a fairy tale with a modern twist.

The wolf is waiting but this time the girl

has more in her basket than goodies.

We want her to kill him

and she is going to do it.

The mind never tires of reenactment.

And revenge, well, when the girl walks out

into the cold night, triumphant,

streaked in the animal's blood,

we warm our hands by that fire.

Renaissance Collection

The Madonna is clean as a sterilized bottle,

unblemished, her face lowered

as though looking at her hands.

In some scenes she is being visited

by the angel who tells of the seed

she will carry in her body.

In others she is holding the baby.

She has a look that tells us

she's been told she's lovely

but doesn't quite believe it.

She'd never catch a glimpse of herself

in the mirror and, what the hell,

undo another button on her blouse,

walk into the interview with hand thrust out

and her breasts like the prow of a ship.

Years later when a girl is born without arms

or with a back that won't straighten,

the doctor hands her over to her father,

man to man. Her father is led

to a private room with a pillow

and a quarter of an hour

to do whatever he thinks is necessary.

How did the girl whose father

couldn't bring himself to smother her

hear this story, who would be the one

to tell her how little she was worth?

Later she'd find her deformity much coveted

by those whose fetishes

encompassed the bizarre, those who wanted

lovers with missing limbs,

provided they were corseted

and rouged to amplify the lack,

those who wanted dwarfs

dressed like Heidi or the woodsman

to walk on their backs.

The rest of us hide our misshapen hearts

like burnt pies. We know the fate

of ugly women. They're the ones relegated

to a life of scraping gum from under the desks

after the children have gone home

while the one whose cheeks are ladles of milk

gets to carry the gold,

give birth to God.

The Tyranny of Beauty

The world is a reflective surface,
a pond, a shop window,
and last night at the party
it was the hard gleam
of a friend's teenage daughter.
Her hair was absurdly shiny
and she kept flinging it over her head,
gathering it in her hands and knotting it
into a crown which stayed in place
for about a minute then fell
like water and the whole process was repeated.
For God's sake, I wanted to say to her,
her tiny brown miniskirt, her long legs,
her tight sweater,
a girl whose sexual self shimmered,
whose boyfriend was the coolest guy there.
He kept his hands around her waist
and tapped his thumbs
against the flatness of her stomach.
I know why old people hate young people.
It's not the music or the fashions
but the terrible mirror of loss.
Her beauty all night made me angry
at the same time that it thrilled me

like an improbable natural wonder.

All night I felt the absence

of that particular power.

I swung between desire—

I wanted to be her, to have her—

and regret,

I was never sixteen

like that.

Beauty is a weapon,

the blade that separates

one girl from another.

We never recover

and it's too late to unlearn

what we spent a lifetime rehearsing.

III

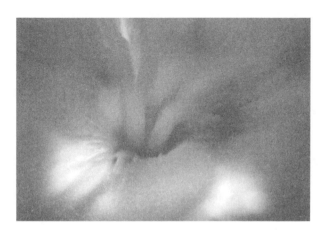

WHAT IS NOT THERE

There is a phone booth by the side of the road
with the light burned out,
you don't have coins
and outside it has begun to rain.
This is where the soul lives.
Its small voice comes
from what sounds like underwater.
Dismantle your life
it says,
you have settled
for too little, though
you may never find more.
You are busy unpacking
in the new house you will come home to
every night, and every night
lie next to the one you have chosen
to ease your weight against.
You will do this for many years,
for as long as it is possible.
The voice sounds like a radio
from the bottom of the lake.
It is announcing news of war,
the conflict of a small country,
a country you think you could locate

on a map, though what you know

of this country is almost nothing.

The body is happy with its good meal,

and the mind with someone to go places with.

The clothes are happy to be piled

on top of each other on the chair,

and the books are content

leaning into each other on the shelves.

But the soul is a bad dog

chained in the yard,

and though there are no intruders,

not even a small animal

rustling in the bushes,

it barks until it wakes you,

wakes the entire neighborhood,

always calling attention

to what is not there,

in the absolute stillness of the night.

WHEN MY LIFE IS ALMOST OVER

Don't humans get to keep one
love from the past alive?
I use mine to remember the body
given over—tulips in a rain storm,
wet all night
and the next morning
their petals torn off
like underclothes.
I think of this love when the dentist
is drilling a tooth
and I want somewhere happy
to go in my mind.
Selective memories,
to be sure, but by the time
my tooth is filled
I am ready to go back
to the sweetness of that tortured life.
Maybe I am living wrong,
settling for tenderness
and the steady bloom.
I want my real life to identify itself,
none of this
having to guess
how I'll feel in the end.
In advance, I say this to my death-bed self:
I squandered my time,

accommodated
fear when I should
have pushed through.
But I couldn't do it,
couldn't throw myself
onto a speeding train.
I chose comfort,
a seat by the window, watching
the green hills roll past.
Easy for you to say
I should have lived harder, better.
You've forgotten
what the middle feels like, years
of painting the living room,
choosing furniture
to go with gold walls.
Marrying kindness
because there are so many
mornings to wake up to.
Now that you are close enough
to feel the heat of the end fires,
only a few coins left in your palm,
you imagine a life of heightened
moments, why couldn't I
have lived like that?
Remember the slowness
of a Thursday,
true, it passes quickly,
but a morning can be unfolded no faster.

Mostly I forget about you,
forget that I will be accountable,
but even when I remember, what do I change?
I will disappoint you,
however I spend
my purse.

What Must Be Loved

Sometimes after we've been,
if not fighting
then having one of those hard talks
that seem to pull us further in
rather than release us,
sometimes after that
when we make love
I want you to slip your fingers
under my skin,
loosen me from my cage of bones
or chip me like gold leaf
off a porcelain shepherdess
with your fingernail.
I bestow upon sex the power
to lift me, like a crane
hoisting a car from the bottom of a lake,
out of my grid of sorrow and lack.
After our hard talk
we let our bodies fall
into each other, slow
as snowflakes drifting
through streetlight
or urgent, pulling
each other back

into the place we share.
Still, the outline
that distinguishes your body
from mine always returns
and it's our two lives
side by side in bed
that must be loved.

HELD

After a night of distance,
each on our own side of the bed,
desire pulls you from sleep,
has you prowling the apartment,
straining like a dog at the end of his lead.
Once they learn the word
children apply it to everything—
they *need* juice or cookies,
need the plastic soldier, the doll
that pees. We learn early
that passion is the gravity
that holds us to our lives.
We move like trains
along the rails, plowing
deeper and deeper into the story.
Rational thought would have turned back
a long time ago, look at how
we make each other suffer.
But sometimes I like to be pinned down,
pressed like a flower between the pages
of a heavy book, a bit of my pigment
rubbing off on them,
their weight holding me down.

UNFAITHFUL

My friend Charlotte is arguing in favor of those
who rub the stone of memory smooth
and have no intention of moving on, getting over.
I feel like I am talking to the nineteenth century.
Pining is a word that can no longer
be said without irony
and ours is a generation of navigators,
adhering to the principles of movement and growth.
A few days later Charlotte tells me
it's not obsession
she admires, but eccentricity,
people who fall in love with the tree
outside their window
and for this reason never move
though the floor in their flat is sagging,
the rooms impossible to heat.
A woman who holds aloft the memory
of the man who briefly loved her
in her twenties
and who still sees his image
in the pan of milk
with almond and sugar heating on the stove
is rewarded with the richness
of a life given over to the internal.

Talking this way, I think of you,

the great love of my life.

But I am unfaithful

and am going to marry the man

I met after you, when I could

no longer stand to be alone.

My love for him takes place

alongside my love for you.

But like the eccentrics

I too have rooms devoted to memory

that save me

from the muscular intimacy

of the actual.

ADDICTIONS OF STRICTNESS

Girls who refuse
all sustenance but air
and water are obsessed
with the body
they want to be rid of.
Food is the sin
of their religion.
The bread of the soul is black,
the milk is curdled.

It is good to leash the animal,
to gain pleasure from the harness.
It has always felt like someone
other than me
giving the orders.
The illusion of being controlled
is seductive
beyond the truth
of controlling.

So when I met you—
how thin and light
and how good you were—
it was natural

to turn you into the one
in charge.

You loved my body
but there were other parts
of me to change.
Sitting at the hard table,
we ate a meal of words,
my portion was guilt
and yours, salvation.

The faithful are afraid
of the wilderness
and follow
down to the last gram
any program of denial.
It is a comfort
to be held
so tightly.

Sacrifice
and passion
are wound together.
The holiest pilgrims
crawl rather than walk.

I was a believer
but always cheated
a little bit

on the program,

rehearsing

what I ought to say

but hiding the rest

like bags of candy

behind the laundry soap

or at the bottom of a drawer of socks.

Rupture

It is easier to be left
than to leave,
the one, a whiplash of pain,
the other, a decision
that may take years to make.
In the months that follow, though,
it is easier being the one
who made the decision.
True, there's the sudden smallness
of your life—where did your house go,
the rooms flooded with afternoon light,
the view of the bay?
True, that first apartment post breakup
is a shocker, aptly named utility,
it gets the job done,
a good place for fear,
what have I done?
and *maybe nothing better*
will come my way.
And a good place for guilt,
I ruin everything I touch.
But the first months of being left
are devoted to the horizontal,
hours on the bed or floor,

weeping and shuffling the deck of memory.
The traveling theater of pain
arrives in every city of the body:
heart and belly, but also feet,
and back of the neck, and knees
from carrying a sack of cement
all day in your arms.
Still, if I had to choose
between leaving or being left,
I would take the blow of rejection
and have gone so far
as to make myself impossible
to live with so my beloved
in the end was the one to leave.
There is nothing admirable
about insisting on the bottom.
I made you do the leaving,
though it's true,
what you accused me of
in the last hateful conversation
we had by phone—
that I had left you,
bit by bit, until finally
you were standing in an empty room
and what else could you do,
good god,
but turn out the lights and go?

The Snake Handler

So now you have met someone new
and tell me over the phone:
she's normal and secure.
Normalcy is highly overrated
among us freaks
I don't say, but think,
to distance myself from the knife.
Too late.
It enters and I carry it all week
between heart and bone.
How long does it take
to understand our lives?
The slow sift,
days of sorrow
followed by those of calm.
Eating my week-day lunch
in the park between classes,
I study the yellow maple
that flares against November's grey.
A blade of beauty
and feeling opens.
That night I dream of the snake handler.
Usually snakes cover the floor
and I am stranded on the bed.

But this time the handler holds them,
one by one, close to my face.
I look into their eyes
and my own reptilian brain,
ruled by the impulse to run
or attack,
acknowledges its kin.

THE COUNTRY OF GRIEF

I have walked across the country of grief.
It took a year.
Mountains went on for months,
the air thin and harsh.
I was ill-equipped for the climb,
though each range prepared me
for the one that followed.
I began to learn where rock
gave a little, my hands
feeling for a place to hold,
my feet for where they could
sink their weight.
There was also,
as one would expect,
desert,
every shade of silver white,
bone, bleached sky.
And you were with me
the whole time,
of course,
like wind in the trees.
I carried the absence of you
which became a kind of presence,
field after field of this,

across fall and into winter.

Then there were the cities.

In a foreign country one is almost happily

a stranger, the busy world

passes as though it were a movie,

nothing solid,

and narrated in a language

the traveler cannot understand.

But I could sit for hours at a little table

in the square, a glass of wine

or a book, something

to hold on to while the world

moved over me.

Grief is a long country

but it does not take a lifetime to cross,

rather, we have time

to cross it many times.

I didn't recognize the moment

I made it out,

the border behind me,

only gradually did I notice

how gentle the air had become

and how hours slipped into each other,

blurred and barely felt in their passing.

I'll tell you, I almost miss

the richness of that year,

pressed up against

the starkness of being.
Grief is a country of white stone,
winter light, mountains
hard and flat in the distance.
Without the wildness of loss,
alone feels natural and plain.
But I like to remember
where I went
and how much
of myself I saw there.

Years Later

The past, so happy to live
in the cave of the mind,
does not exist when bumped into at the street fair,
only the person who lived there with you,
whose physical presence now only saddens
because the person you remember,
the one whose image had a nightly run
in the theater of private thoughts
for so long after you parted,
that one is gone
and in his place
the man who carried on without you,
who went back to school, graduated,
got new friends, shaved his head—
a look you would have strongly
advised him against
had you still been in a position to do so.
The moment of reunion is never as graceful
in real life as it is in fantasy.
You are eating a skewer of grilled meat
so part of your attention goes to wondering
if you have barbeque sauce on your cheek.
You are glad when the moment is over,
when you are finished saying

whatever awkward words come to you
and now you can watch him disappear
back into the crowd
because the past, like a fish
yanked from the lake on a line,
cannot live outside its own element.
Its quick gleam goes back under
and the surface of the lake,
pearly green in June,
seals over without so much as a scar
to show where the tear was made.
Later you will drink scotch with a friend,
it tastes like woods and mist
in its glass with ice,
and after your friend has gone,
loss will settle around you.
There's nothing wrong with feeling
a little sad drunk.
Take off your clothes,
lower yourself into the bath,
let the steam rise off you,
the heat loosen the ropes
and the heart float out on its raft.

IV

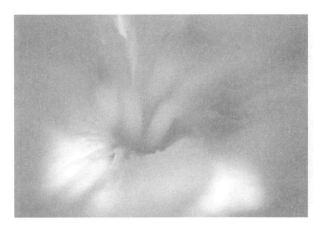

Safe Sex

The girl, born in the '70s,
confesses that she doesn't
do safe sex.
Oh, she makes a half-hearted attempt,
but at some point both she
and the guy—
he's lanky and has learned
how to dress his height—
stop unrolling the condom,
the way an earlier generation of lovers
moved from kissing to fondling,
from breasts to genitals.
Every generation takes on
and then rejects the edicts of restriction.
Hers came of age in plague time
and has learned to navigate danger.
Mostly the girl is rocked to sleep
in the cradle of low risk,
though sometimes terror
blazes in her chest
deep in the fear hours of night.
What she really wants is faith
that one body brings goodness to another.
Discussing the topic in class,

my students won't hear of it

and regale me with stories,

their voices high with excitement:

guys can't be trusted,

girls can't be trusted,

let me tell you what happened to my cousin.

I don't tell them how I do it.

Like the girl in the essay

we've been reading,

my lover and I moved closer

into each other's lives and then let

the barrier slip,

barrier which I'm inclined to believe

for many of us

has less to do with prevention

than with distance,

a kind of sexual formality,

like the shift in language

that changes a man

from *someone I'm seeing*

to *my beloved.*

My students are right,

it is dangerous, even crazy,

to walk out into that thin air unsheathed.

MY REAL LIFE

Years from now I may tell someone
I married my husband
for the wrong reason.
Afraid of my own life,
I couldn't bear my singular
existence.
The one I will tell,
perhaps my oldest friend,
but maybe a woman I just met
at a conference,
has her own long story of love.
The best stories change
every time we tell them,
fluid as glass turning back
into sand or fire,
a looser form of matter.
Even as a child I knew
I would live my life alone.
I married my husband
to cheat fate
I tell the woman at the conference
on that mild winter day in the future.
We are doing what an earlier generation
would have called confessing.

She has a lover
her husband
must know about.
She tells herself
this season she will leave
one man or the other.
We have pulled our chairs to the edge
of the deck and can see out
across the mountains.
Far into our stories,
we are trying to move beyond
the rehearsed versions
we've said so often
we no longer know
if they're true.
At night we are back on the deck,
looking at stars,
glasses of wine in our hands.
I married my husband—
the words are phosphorous as waves—
because I wanted
to enter the small room of intimacy
and live there with a man.
I wanted to know how far
love could get inside me
and I wanted to know
where I would not let it go.

Will I tell my new friend

that I have never stopped

being uncertain,

or will I say that finally,

somewhere around the fifth year,

I settled into my life—

my new life,

the one that is broken open,

so far from the sealed

version I imagined as a child?

I hope I will tell my friend

that I am happy,

that it was the right choice

saying yes to my husband's

generous love

and that I can no longer

imagine any other ending.

THE GUEST LIST

I imagine the guests arriving,
some pulling packages
out of the trunks of their cars,
then walking across the parking lot
to the place I will be married,
finding a seat next to others they know.
They look good on this August evening
in their nice clothes,
and if one were to eavesdrop on a conversation
over the buffet, it would likely be interesting,
intelligent, something to do with art
or the nature of being human
at this particular time.
But when I think about my friends
and family, I am also afraid.
How do I exist in the private
quarters of their minds,
in those dark rooms where we all
sometimes wish mild failure
on others so that we might shine.
And they, in fairness, should fear me,
though I will greet them
with open arms, genuinely pleased
they could make it.

I want to wear a fancy dress

and have everyone see me

the moment I admit

I trust another person

with my life,

though some of my guests

might be thinking

that I look old or fat

or that my new husband does,

or that they do in the outfit they never

should have bought, what made them think

they looked good in aqua?

The mind wanders back to the familiar

constrictions of sorrow.

So be it. We are frail as a handful of snow.

And it is not enough to choose one person

to love, we must make lists

of everyone we want

to hold our lives in place.

THE FLOOR

All week we carry
the old dog outside to pee
and bathe him on the deck
in the sun when we are too late.
My beloved brings a bucket of warm water
from the sink, dips the cloth and lathers the dog.
Belief is beside the point.
If the universe is full of meaning
or empty, what difference?
The dog is wobbly, suffering
from what the vet called *geriatric vestibula.*
Vestibule
of the inner ear
that welcomes the world into the body
as a winter traveler, leaving the chilly station,
briefly warms herself in the entrance
before sliding open the door,
finding her seat on the train.
An infection or a small stroke,
and the calm sea of balance
sloshes over. We steady
the dog until the floor is level
and the room stops spinning.
Once I loved a man with no furniture.
A year after his divorce he was still living

out of boxes. We ate on the bed,
using an atlas as a table.
There is a map to everywhere,
only a matter of finding it,
and he was determined
to survey his life,
every landscape cleared,
the honeycombed heart cleaned out.
But to sit quietly with suffering
as beside a creek one has walked a long way
to reach, to lie back on a rock in the sun
and to breathe the sweet, green water,
to feel how grief given enough room
softens, this I learned later
when my heart was more than broken,
was powdered, coarse sand
the body gone through fire
turns into.
Every day now
we are on the floor with the dog.
I like it here where it's cool
and where the crumbs of our meals have fallen,
and hair and fur,
what is usually far below us,
once only the bottoms of my feet
but now my whole body
a citizen of this other world
of what is dropped and lost.

Every Morning

Looking out, early winter,
into the dark green branches
of the cedar and to the light
that lives among them,
I see it is not about being ready
but being ready enough
and then doing teaches us how.
I imagine my parents
not being ready when I was born.
All they could do at first
was keep me warm and fed.
We devote ourselves,
though we have no idea
what it means
to stay that long.
Let's say one has decided to meditate
every morning or to write
when the house is quiet
and the rooms are dark blue and seem
themselves still drifting in sleep.
Go to your cushion or desk,
notice yourself standing there
and then notice walking
either toward or away from

the life you have said you want.

This is commitment,

my friend Lynn suggested.

Though if it is a baby in her crib

it is not possible to turn away,

you have, though we hate

to hear these words,

no choice

but to lower your arms into the dark,

lift her from a foam of covers

and carry her to the window,

warm your chest with her body

and point out the moon,

pretending she is not too young to care.

She is not too young to care,

only the word moon and even the thing itself

must mean many things because she cannot

hold a dozen nouns,

so moon is your breathing chest

and the sweet milk inside it,

and moon is the shadowy shapes

of bears and ponies on the shelves

and the feeling in the room of close and good.

No one asks us if we want

to live our whole lives,

every day taking up the work of the self.

How many mornings will I wake

in the still dark,
light the stove, make coffee,
open the door for the dog
who, sleep-soft,
has risen from his bed
and needs to go out?

Acknowledgments

Poems from this book first appeared in the following journals:

Kalliope: "Evening News"
Nimrod: "Prayer"
New Millennium: "The Warmest Day of the Year"
Runes: "The Snake Handler"
San Francisco Bay Guardian: "Lexicon" and "What Is Not There"

I want to thank Melody Lacina, Sharon Fain, Laura Horn,
C.B. Follett, Sandy Nicholls, Susan Terris, and Ella Eytan
for their valuable comments on many of these poems.
Thanks also to Lynn Crawford for inspiration and to my
teacher Chana Bloch for her ongoing support.
To my husband, Jeff Erickson, thank you for the pleasures
of home. I am grateful to my family who taught me the
power and weight of belonging. And, in memory,
to Buster—my muse and my companion.